My Discontent

poems

Joseph Hart

Cyberwit.net
HIG 45 Kaushambi Kunj, Kalindipuram
Allahabad - 211011 (U.P.) India
http://www.cyberwit.net
Tel: +(91) 9415091004
E-mail: info@cyberwit.net

You've got to be taught

You've got to be taught
To be afraid
Of people whose eyes
Are oddly made
And people whose skin
Is a different shade.
You've got to be carefully taught.
You've got to be taught
To hate and fear.
You've got to be taught
From year to year.
It's got be drummed
In your dear little ear.
You've got to be carefully taught.
You've got to be taught
Before it's too late,
Before you are 6
Or 7 or 8
To hate all the people
Your relatives hate.
You've got to be carefully taught.
You've got to be carefully taught.

- Oscar Hammerstein II

"There's got to be a morning after..."

"And much it grieves my heart to see
What man has done to man."

- William Wordsworth

Man brings to completion
The grief his Gods began.

"Why do you prate so about God? Everything you say about him is wrong."

"Don't be so blinded by your morals that you fail to do what's right."

- Isaac Asimov

Contents

Man

Once I had a magazine -
"The Wonders Man Has Done" -
Architecture, statues,
The Parthenon, Cathedrals.
Someone took my magazine,
Creased it in the middle
And used it as a funnel to
Pour pot into a pipe.

Gold

Fifty years of marriage
And the vase was gold.
She loved it.
After many years,
Her husband died and she
And the vase were old.
In a home –
The past was far away.
She'd probably forgotten -
The gilded vase was sold -
But not for much.
Memories don't pay.

Mr. Liston

Mr. Liston was intelligent -
Considerably so,
Clever, gentle, kind.
He was a teacher.
Yesterday I saw him
After he was old -
Crippled, with a
Constant, mindless smile.

Truths

The followers of Darwin
Dig up bones that show
The truths of evolution.
Does this make it so?

Christians think they have
Another truth as well.
Despite how deep they dig,
They'll never find a hell.

The universe has edges.
Light is particles and waves.
None of them a truth
At the bottom of old graves.

Cats

A cat will sit and stare at you -
Stare and stare and stare at you -
Neither smile nor glare at you -
Just stare and stare and stare -

Gun Rights

If they go to heaven,
They'll go alone.
Republicans have
A heart of stone.

The murder of children
That someone loved
Leaves conservatives
Hard, unmoved.

They all see angels
In the sky
And do not care
When people die.

"There are angels
In the sky" -
That's not a hymn -
It's a battle cry.

My Father

All sense of reality
Left behind -
Hallucinations – I was scared.
If he'd known
What was in my mind,
Would he have cared?

A Riddle

I heard a little riddle.
I don't remember when.
You believe there's nothing
Your deity can't do.
Can he make a rock
So big that he can't lift it?
You say - "That's only words."
Then answer me with words.

Freddy's Walk

Before, like all the others, we are dead,
I have a little cat. His name is Fred,
Who like a phantom moves upon the bed
In a silent, stationary tread.

Truth

Looking for a Truth
To sew on pillow cases -
The Theory of Relativity – or sex:
The 7 minute substitute for God -

Then

In little English houses
In parlors with pianos
They listened to sweet music
While reading poetry.

Tennyson and Byron -
Books with gilt-edge pages -
And someone played piano -
Chopin – and this was art.

Lines

His father was a drunk,
An addict and a Nazi.
He beat his son.
And when the boy was 10,
He found his father's gun
And shot him in the head.
Arrested and convicted -
What became of him?
Forgotten now. And where
Is right or understanding,
Justice or a God?

Names

I changed my name in 83
To escape the past
And the madness in it.
Now it seems – for 40 years -
I have no name at all.
The old name is too painful
And the new one isn't me.
No name on my headstone, just
"No one's buried here."

Lines

Cut up a republican,
Examine every part.
You'll find a soul – a holy one.
But you won't find a heart.

Souls

To see a little life go out -
It's too much to believe!
To watch a little light go out
Once where there was love.
Many many animals
On earth since life began -
Do all of them have souls?
Why not, if people do?

The Sky

A million million millions
Stare with longing at the sky.
Pianists get old,
And even poets die.

Kill!

Kill – kill – kill
Animals and and men!
Spare the dogs and cats because they're cute.
Kill! Kill! Kill!
Kill and kill again!
Sing in church and then go out and shoot!

Thoughts

If people thought
What I thought they were thinking,
They would be crazy,
And I would be sane.

Lines

God and evolution -
Neither one seems right -
A hundred birds
Flying in formation -
That idiosyncratic beast:
A cat.

The Bird

I heard a little bird
Singing almost right.
I taught it how to sing
And then one furtive night
It never sang again.
Now all I hear is rain.

Endgame

Resurrecting time,
Nothing ever changes.
Don't argue with a Caesar;
What he wants is going to happen.

Now the world is ending
(Not a whimper but a bang) -
And nothing is important –
Not emperors or Keats.

The Wall

What can be beyond
The wall?
It's sobering to think
There is no God at all.

A Song

No world but this one -
No love but a cat -
And when I die,
That's that.

But when I hear
The charm of a song,
I feel the skeptics
Are wrong.

Lines

One needn't be old-fashioned
To like a pretty song.
But it takes a talent
To compose one.
Since centuries the world
Has liked a pretty tune.
Now the world is weary
And after something new:
Ugliness - that's not a tune at all.

Treasures

The treasures in my room -
Hamelin and Proust -
Pictures on the walls -
Curios on the shelves -

Fastened to the world -
Unable to break free -
Are everything to me -
And indifferent to you -

Lines

Amazing that this bigot
With a swagger and a gun
Was once a little child who never
Hated any one.

The Sin

The sin that worries Christians,
(And to which their God objects)
That they holler from the pulpit,
Is sex.

All the world's a bedroom
To stick their noses in.
To a proper Christian
There's no other sin.

Fred

Little cat
What do you see
When you stare
So long at me?

Can it be
As Shakespeare said
That the beasts
Have an empty head?

For several minutes
You sit and stare
Before you jump
Onto the chair.

Lines

Can talent be extinct?
Can genius be passe?
The world wants mediocrity,
And that is what it's getting.

Music without melodies
And poems with no art -
Beauty's very fragile
And easily destroyed.

Where's another Renaissance?
The artists of today
With no inhibitions
Are turning gold to straw.

Lines

For a thousand thousand years
Emperors and kings
Were regarded as a deity,
And afterlife a fact.

The beauty and the nonsense
Imagination brings!
Let me go to heaven
While my mind's intact.

My Grandmother

She brutalized my Grandma
Who didn't speak,
But clenched her jaw
And just looked far away.
Did this ease the pain?
It didn't stop the words.
Now both of them are dead
And it is over.

Kitty

I pushed him off my chest
With an angry shove.
I thought that he felt pleasure,
And not love.

I think I was insane,
Thinking, doing that.
Not crazy – I was evil.
Kitty was a cat.

Sartre & Camus

Sartre & Camus – were just two men
Who looked around and thought,
"Is there a God? Or a loving God?
Obviously not."

The Gods

Watch with wild-eyed horror
As earth endures its fate.
Why complain and hate the Gods?
There are no Gods to hate.

Dinosaurs & Flies

I don't believe that love
Is a thing of evolution.
Nor that a world of animals
Was put on earth for men.

Life

Don't believe you're safe
And myths of God are true.
They murdered Oscar Wilde,
And they'll murder you.

Beauty

Will scientists discover
Phantoms in the sky?
I know when something's beautiful,
But I don't know why.

Beauty's only beautiful.
It has no truths to tell.
Poets have so much to say
They needn't say it well.

The philistines have won.
Why continue fretting?
The world wants mediocrity,
And that is what it's getting.

The Yank

I'm a gun totin', faggot hatin',
Patriot yank.
I put my trust in Jesus
And my money in the bank.

Lines

Read the poetry of Keats
To get a new sensation.
Religions are a testament
To sweet imagination.

The Catatonic

How statuelike I see thee stand,
Sitting in a chair,
Not saying anything,
Not going anywhere;
No expression but a stare.

Laughed the smug psychologist,
"So what if he's insane?
Anyway he's happy."
Though no one could explain,
Then said the catatonic,
"I'm in constant pain."

Americans

Americans take selfies -
Laugh at universities -
Give themselves a high five -
And think Monet's a beer.

"MAGA"

"Make America Great Again."
Backward we shall go
To the days of Joe McCarthy -
The evil of Jim Crow -
Keeping gays in closets -
And women's status low -

Lines

Philosophy and physics -
I do not understand them.
I know a little Broadway;
This is all.

Philosophy is interesting.
Science is the Truth.
Sculptors and composers
And painters – this is art.

Lines

It takes a great intelligence
To write a string quartet -
And talented
To make the music sing.

Technology

The ones who make technology
Are geniuses – and they
Also made the bombs
To blow it all away.

The Songwriter

Coward they called "the master".
He called him "the master of blather".
And Merman who sang in Gershwin,
Porter and Berlin and Styne -
He called her "a stupid dog".
That is what he said.
"Infinite talent but limited soul"
And "infinite soul but limited talent"
Were Rodgers and Hammerstein.
That's what he said.
That's what he said.
This from a man who
Was lost in music,
With perfectly adequate words -
Not great and not the best -
Others so very much better -
But perfectly adequate words.

1971

Dennis went for help.
The clinic was unreal.
Everyone deferred
To a performing seal.

Dennis went away.
No one said to wait.
I later read he jumped
From the Golden Gate.

In matters such as this
No one blames the shrink.
The fault must lie with Dennis
Floating in the drink.

Hell

I made a list of the evil I've done -
And the list is long.
But Hitler, Putin and
Donald Trump
Await a hell that's hotter -
Though if they think
There is no hell,
Probably they're right.

Freddy

My little cat will stare
For minutes without blinking
While I sit in a chair.
I don't know what he's thinking.

Can it be that he
Wants to be like me?
Wonders why I love him?
Or wonders what I am?

Shrinks

Avoid the psychotherapists!
Jesus Christ! They're vicious!
They'll tell you you're a queer,
Ridiculous and
Shit comes from your mouth.
Ask for explanations -
You won't get an answer.
Stay alone and crazy -
It's less painful.

The World

"Alternate facts! " "Alternate facts!"
Full-grown men believe it.
Though Russia is attacking,
The aggressor is the victim.
Jesus in the schools
Is shoved down little throats.
In spite of all the other Gods -
Or even none at all.
The bigots and the racists
Are shown what they are doing
And do it anyway.
What's become of art?
Unwanted and forgotten!
The world wants mediocrity,
And that is what it's getting.
Dylan, Stephen Sondheim
And Putin – what's the use?

Diagnosis

In my soul a platform or a floor -
Above it total insincerity -
I don't like the people that I like -
Beneath it sewage, sludge and what I feel
And the whole of my intelligence-

Things

Beethoven, Alkan and Bach,
Hamelin, Cziffra and Smith,
Ashkenzay and Wild -
The poetry I've read -
Horowitz who's dead -

Beautiful beautiful things!
Beautiful - although
Will anyone remember
When they're long ago?
This can't be so.

JS

She asked if she had answered all my questions.
I hadn't written her for 7 years.
And I hadn't asked her any questions.
She sent it to a name she didn't know.
I had changed my name in 83.
And to an address that she didn't have.
Would anyone have answered such a letter?
I didn't answer her. I was afraid.
She drove me crazy once. And I felt guilty
For all of it. And here she was again.

In Oakland

I was sitting in a coffee shop
Smoking cigarettes
With a cup of coffee.
Two therapists came in.
I don't know how they knew
Where I was or when I'd be there.
They telephoned the cops
Who came and with a smile
Said, "We heard you're suicidal
And we want to help."
I thought he meant they wanted
To help me kill myself.
The cops took me away.
They drove me to a mental ward
And told me to get out,
Go anywhere I liked;
And then they drove away.
Maybe if I'd asked -
So very long ago -
I take my medication -
Can the madness come again?

Friends

Grandpa and Johnny and Maxx,
Freddy and Kitty, too,
Leo and Nermal and Smoe -
Love is sweet when it's true.

Christianity

A nice and gentle man
Tells you he's a God;
Believe him
And heaven's in the bag.
Doubt it and you're doomed.
So very simple.
Regardless what you do -
Homicide or rape -
Has really no importance
So long as you believe.
Theology, cathedrals
And a couple thousand years
Of saints and books and martyrs
Are flowers on a grave.

Christians

The first Christians
Were thrown to the beasts.
Their God did not protect them.
That would occasion
It seems at least
To question if not reject him.

Pagans

Sitting in the winter
In the silence of my flat
Contemplating pagans
While I hold my sleeping cat -
The aim of Christ – the Christians really
Made a mess of that.
All the ancient deities
Are old and rather worn.
From the womb of heresy
Will another God be born?